Materials

Rubber

Cassie Mayer

Heinemann Library
Chicago, Illinois

Customer Service 888-454-2279
Visit our website at www.heinemannraintree.com

Picture research: Tracy Cummins and Heather Mauldin
Designed by Joanna Hinton-Malivoire
Printed in the United States of America in North Mankato, Minnesota.   072015   009094RP

17 16 15
10 9 8 7 6 5

ISBN-13: 978-1-4329-1621-3 (hc)
ISBN-13: 978-1-4329-1630-5 (pb)

The Library of Congress has cataloged the first edition as follows:
Mayer, Cassie.
  Rubber / Cassie Mayer.
     p. cm. -- (Materials)
  Includes bibliographical references and index.
  ISBN 978-1-4329-1621-3 (hc) -- ISBN 978-1-4329-1630-5 (pb) 1. Rubber--Juvenile literature. I. Title.
  TS1890.M358 2008
  620.1'94--dc22
                            2008005581

Acknowledgments
The author and publisher are grateful to the following for permission to reproduce copyright material: ©Corbis p. **4** (Getty Images/AFP/Mark Ralston, p. **15** (Remi Benali/Corbis); ©Getty Images p. **7** (Richard Drury); ©Heinemann Raintree pp. **6**, **9**, **11**, **17**, **18**, **19**, **20**, **21**, **22** (David Rigg); ©Istockphoto p. **10** (Justin Horrocks); ©Peter Arnold p. **12** (Mark Edwards); ©Shutterstock pp. **5** (Geir Olav Lyngfjell), **8** (Perov Stanislav), **13** (Cecilia Lim H M), **14** (Marco Rametta), **16** (Feverpitched), **23** (Marco Rametta).

Cover image used with permission of ©agefotostock (Stephanie Adams). Back cover image used with permission of ©Heinemann Raintree (David Rigg).

Contents

What Is Rubber?

Rubber is made by people.

Rubber is used by people.

Rubber can be strong.

Rubber can be weak.

Rubber can be hard.

Rubber can be soft.

Rubber can bounce.

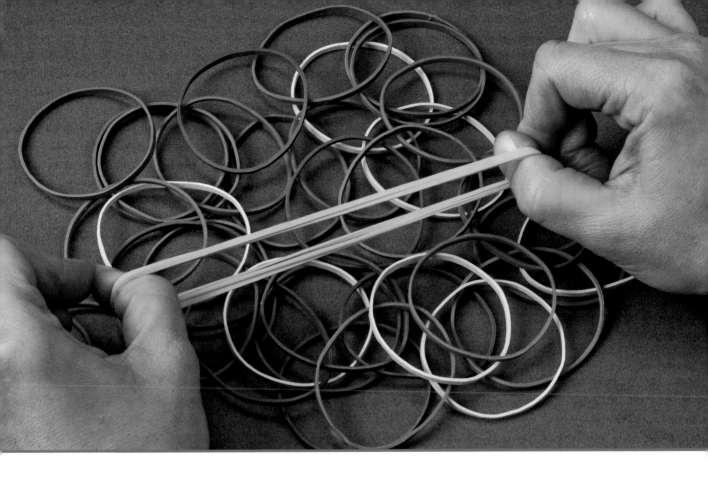

Rubber can stretch.

Making Rubber

Rubber can be made by people.

rubber tree

Rubber can be made from things in nature.

Rubber can be made from tree sap.

Rubber can be made from oil.

How Do We Use Rubber?

Rubber can be used to make hoses.

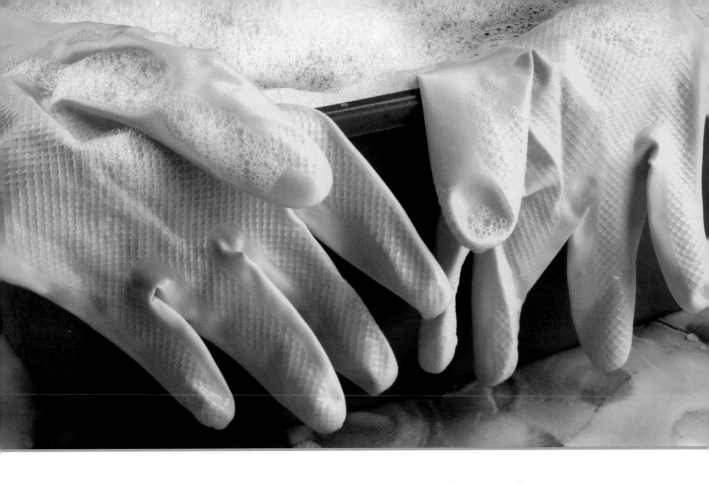

Rubber can be used to make gloves.

Rubber can be used to make tires.

Rubber can be used to make toys.

Rubber can be used to make shoes.

Rubber can be used to make
many things.

Things Made of Rubber

▲tire

▲rubber eraser

▲rubber toy

▲rubber shoe

Picture Glossary

sap thick liquid that comes from trees

Content Vocabulary for Teachers

material Something that takes up space and can be used to make other things

natural resource material found in nature that can be used by people

Index

Note to Parents and Teachers

Before reading

Ask children what they know about rubber. Can they think of any objects made from rubber? If they have trouble brainstorming, help them think about objects used indoors, such as rubber bands, toys, and rubber erasers.

After reading

• Place a variety of rubber objects in front of children and ask them to sort the items into groups. Use diverse objects with different colors, textures, and sizes. Then, ask the children to write a list of descriptive words for each group.

• Give children a rubber object, such as a rubber toy, and a non-rubber object, such as a wooden toy. Then, ask children to compare the appearance, weight and texture of the two different objects.